UNLOCKING THE POWER OF YOUR SMARTPHONE:
Easy ways to make Money Online

Donn L. Taylor

Table of contents

Chapter1

Introduction:

In today's fast-paced digital era, smartphones have become an integral part of our daily lives. From communication and entertainment to accessing information and staying connected, smartphones have unlocked immense power and potential. However, what if I told you that your smartphone can also be a gateway to making money online? Yes, you read that right. With the right strategies and techniques, you can leverage your smartphone to create additional income streams and unlock financial opportunities.

In this comprehensive guide, we will explore a wide range of practical and effective methods to harness the potential of your smartphone. Whether you're a tech-savvy individual looking to maximize your smartphone's capabilities or someone new to the online money-making realm, this guide will equip you with the knowledge and tools necessary to embark on your journey to financial success.

"Easy Ways to Make Money Online," encapsulates the main objective of this guide - to provide you with simple yet impactful methods to generate income through your smartphone. We understand that not everyone has hours to spare or specialized skills, which is why we have curated a collection of straightforward techniques that can be easily implemented by anyone, regardless of their technological background or prior experience.

In the upcoming sections, we will delve into various proven strategies, including online freelancing, app-based income opportunities, affiliate marketing, and more. We will discuss each method in detail, providing step-by-step instructions, tips, and tricks to ensure your success. Moreover, we will also address common challenges and pitfalls, giving you insights on how to navigate potential obstacles along the way.

About Smartphones and their Power:

Ultimately, the aim of this guide is to empower you to tap into the remarkable potential of your smartphone and leverage it as a tool for financial growth. By implementing the strategies outlined in this book, you can unlock a world of opportunities, allowing you to earn money online conveniently, on your terms, and without the need for significant financial investments. With dedication and an open mind, you can transform your smartphone from a mere device into a valuable asset that contributes to your financial well-being.

So, are you ready to take control of your smartphone's potential and embark on a journey towards financial independence? Let's dive into the world of online money-making, discover the easy ways to make money using your smartphone, and unlock your path to financial success.

Smartphones have revolutionized numerous aspects of our lives, and one area where they have an immense impact is in the realm of making money online. As our smartphones have become more advanced and feature-rich, they have opened up countless opportunities for individuals to generate income without the constraints of traditional work settings. Here, I will delve into some of the ways smartphones empower users to make money online.

First and foremost, smartphones provide easy access to a plethora of online marketplaces and platforms. Whether it's e-commerce giant platforms like Amazon or popular freelance platforms like Upwork, smartphones allow individuals to seamlessly connect with a global audience and find various work opportunities.

Users can effortlessly create profiles, browse job listings, communicate with clients, and complete tasks, all through the convenience of their handheld device. This accessibility extends to various industries, including writing, graphic design, coding, virtual assistance, and many others, enabling individuals to monetize their skills and expertise effectively.

Moreover, smartphones enable users to leverage the power of social media platforms to monetize their online presence. With the rise of influencers and content creators, social media has become an avenue for individuals to showcase their talents, build a following, and subsequently monetize their online presence. Through apps like Instagram, YouTube, TikTok, and Twitter, individuals can engage with their audience, promote products or services, secure sponsorships, and generate revenue through advertisements or collaborations. Smartphones, with their built-in cameras and media editing capabilities, provide the necessary tools for individuals to create and share compelling content that resonates with their audience.

Furthermore, smartphones empower users to participate in the gig economy, which has grown exponentially in recent years. Apps and platforms like Uber, Lyft, TaskRabbit, and Fiverr connect individuals with various gig opportunities, allowing them to earn money on their terms. Whether it's providing ride-sharing services, completing household tasks, or offering specialized skills, smartphones serve as the gateway for accessing and managing these gig opportunities. The flexibility and convenience provided by smartphones enable users to seamlessly work on their own schedule, expanding their earning potential and fostering a more independent work-life balance.

In addition to these opportunities, smartphones play a significant role in enabling online entrepreneurship. Mobile apps have democratized the process of starting and running a business, offering individuals the means to create and manage their own ventures. From launching an e-commerce store using platforms like Shopify or Etsy, to developing and selling mobile applications, smartphones provide the necessary tools to conceptualize, execute, and monitor a business venture. The ubiquity of smartphones and the ease of access to the internet have eliminated many barriers to entry, allowing budding entrepreneurs to turn their ideas into profitable realities.

However, while smartphones offer immense opportunities for making money online, it is crucial to acknowledge that success in this realm requires diligence, skill, and adaptability.

Building a strong online presence, establishing a credible reputation, and continually honing one's skills are key factors in generating sustainable income. Additionally, staying up-to-date with the rapidly evolving landscape of online platforms, algorithms, and trends becomes paramount in order to remain competitive in the online marketplace.

In conclusion, smartphones have become indispensable tools for making money online. They provide individuals with access to a plethora of online platforms, enable the monetization of social media presence, facilitate participation in the gig economy, and empower online entrepreneurship. With the right strategies, dedication, and adaptability, smartphones offer the power to unlock various avenues and create profitable opportunities in the digital realm.

Benefits of Making Money Online:

Making money online has become more accessible and achievable than ever, thanks to the advancements in technology, especially smartphones. These handheld devices have transformed into powerful tools capable of generating income, offering numerous benefits for individuals looking to make money online. Here are some key advantages of using a smartphone for online money-making endeavors:

- 1. Portability and Flexibility: Smartphones allow you to earn money from anywhere at any time. With a smartphone in hand, you have the flexibility to work on your online ventures while traveling, commuting, or even from the comfort of your home. This portability enables you to seize opportunities and make money without being tied to a specific location.

- 2. Broad Range of Money-Making Opportunities: The digital era has provided a vast array of online money-making opportunities, catering to various skills and interests. Whether it's freelancing, online tutoring, content creation, affiliate marketing, or participating in online surveys, smartphones offer a convenient platform to engage in these activities. You can explore different avenues and find the most suitable option to monetize your skills and passions.

- 3. Lower Setup Costs: Compared to traditional brick-and-mortar businesses, the upfront costs of starting an online business or making money online through a smartphone are relatively low. You can find numerous free or affordable apps, platforms, and tools that enable you to kickstart your online venture without significant financial investments.

This affordability reduces the barrier to entry and empowers more individuals to explore online income opportunities.

- 4. Time Efficiency: Smartphones save time by condensing various tasks into a single device. You can manage your online business or money-making activities through productivity apps, communication tools, and automation software, all within the palm of your hand. This convenience allows you to optimize your time, streamline operations, and focus on income-generating tasks without the need for extensive setups or equipment.

- 5. Access to a Global Marketplace: The internet has transformed the world into a global marketplace, and smartphones provide easy access to this vast audience.

- With a smartphone and an internet connection, you can reach potential customers, clients, or employers from different parts of the world. This connectivity expands your earning potential by tapping into larger markets, opening doors to international collaborations, and increasing your chances of earning a substantial income.

- 6. Diverse Revenue Streams: Smartphones enable you to diversify your income streams effortlessly. You can engage in multiple online money-making activities simultaneously, whether it's selling products or services, monetizing your content through ads, or even investing in digital currency. Leveraging your smartphone, you can create a portfolio of income streams, reducing dependence on a single source and increasing your overall earning potential

Smartphones have revolutionized the way we make money online, providing a range of benefits that include flexibility, affordability, global connectivity, and time efficiency. By leveraging the power of smartphones, individuals have the opportunity to explore various online income avenues, tap into a global marketplace, and potentially earn a significant income right from the palm of their hands.

Chapter2

Understanding the Basics:

In the modern era of technological advancements, the internet has not only revolutionized the way we connect with others but also opened up a plethora of opportunities to generate income. Among the various avenues available, making money online using smartphones has emerged as a popular and accessible option for individuals seeking financial flexibility and independence. This article aims to provide an in-depth understanding of the basics of easy ways to make money online, focusing on smartphone-based opportunities.

Smartphones have become indispensable tools in our lives, acting as portals to the digital realm. With their power and connectivity, they offer a host of earning possibilities right at our fingertips. Here are some key areas where smartphones can be leveraged to generate income online:

1. E-commerce: The rise of online marketplaces and platforms has made it easier than ever to start an online business. With a smartphone, individuals can create and manage their own e-commerce store, selling products or services to customers worldwide. This allows entrepreneurs to capitalize on their creative endeavors, tapping into a global customer base without the need for a physical storefront.

2. Freelancing: Smartphones provide a convenient means for freelancers to find and take on remote work opportunities. A plethora of freelance platforms cater to various skill sets, such as writing, graphic design, programming, and virtual assistance. By leveraging their expertise, individuals can actively seek out and complete projects from the comfort of their

own homes, setting their own schedules and earning potential.

3. Content Creation: With the widespread popularity of social media platforms, individuals can utilize their smartphones to create and share engaging content.

Whether it's through blogging, vlogging, or social media influencing, individuals can monetize their content through various means such as brand collaborations, sponsorships, and advertising revenue. The key is to deliver high-quality content that resonates with a targeted audience, building a devoted following over time.

4. Online Surveys and Microtasks: Smartphone apps and websites now offer opportunities to participate in surveys, complete microtasks, or take up short-term gigs for quick payments. These options are ideal for those looking for flexible earning methods without significant time

commitments. While the individual payout may be small, they can add up over time, providing supplementary income.

5. Investment and Trading: Advancements in financial technology have made it easier for individuals to participate in investing and trading activities through smartphone applications. With access to stock trading platforms, cryptocurrency exchanges, and robo-advisors, individuals can engage in wealth-building activities at their convenience.

However, it is crucial to approach this avenue with knowledge and caution, as it carries inherent risks.

It is important to note that making money online, even through smartphones, requires dedication, effort, and continuous learning. Building a sustainable income stream in the online space will likely involve a combination of the aforementioned methods, tailored to individual skills, interests, and goals. Additionally, maintaining professionalism, ethical conduct, and adaptability are key factors in establishing a successful online presence.

In conclusion, smartphones hold immense power when it comes to making money online. The opportunities presented by e-commerce, freelancing, content creation, microtasks, and investment activities make it feasible for individuals to generate income from virtually anywhere, at any time. However, persistence, commitment, and a clear understanding of the chosen avenue are pivotal to achieving financial success in the digital realm.

How to choose the right smartphone:

When it comes to making money online, most or browseable phones are suitable but having the right smartphone can significantly enhance your productivity, efficiency, and overall success. With the myriad of options available in the market, choosing the perfect smartphone for your online endeavors can seem overwhelming. However, by considering a few essential factors, you can make an informed decision that aligns with your specific needs and goals.

1. Operating System:
The first decision you'll have to make is choosing between iOS and Android. Both systems have their advantages, so consider your familiarity and personal preferences. Android offers a wider range of devices and customization options, while iOS offers a seamless integration with other Apple products and a more curated app store.

2. Performance:
To handle the demanding tasks required for online money-making, such as running multiple apps simultaneously or editing multimedia content, opt for a smartphone

with a powerful processor and sufficient RAM. Look for devices powered by the latest generations of processors like Snapdragon or Exynos.

3. Storage:
Sufficient storage is crucial for storing your work-related files, apps, and media. Consider your requirements and opt for a smartphone with ample built-in storage or with the option to expand it through a microSD card.

4. Display and Screen Size:
A large, high-resolution display is beneficial for tasks like content creation, graphic design, or analyzing data. However, it's essential to strike a balance between a comfortable screen size and portability. Look for smartphones with a screen size around 6 inches for a good compromise.

5. Battery Life:

A long-lasting battery is essential, especially if you're frequently working on the go or in areas where power outlets may not be readily available. Look for smartphones with larger battery capacities and fast-charging capabilities to ensure uninterrupted productivity.

6. Camera Quality:
If your online money-making activities involve visuals, prioritizing a smartphone with a high-quality camera is crucial. Look for devices with multiple lenses, higher megapixel counts, and advanced camera features to capture professional-looking photos and videos.

7. Connectivity and Networking:
Ensure that your chosen smartphone supports the latest connectivity standards, such as 4G or 5G, to ensure fast and stable internet access. Additionally, consider devices with dual SIM capabilities if you

need to manage multiple online accounts simultaneously.

8. Security Features:
Protecting your online activities, data, and transactions is paramount. Look for smartphones equipped with biometric authentication features, such as fingerprint scanners or facial recognition, to ensure secure access to your device and sensitive information.

By carefully considering these factors, you can choose a smartphone that meets your specific requirements and maximizes your ability to generate income online. Remember, investing in a high-quality smartphone tailored to your needs can be a worthwhile investment that enhances your overall productivity and success in the digital realm.

Essential Apps for Making Money Online:

When it comes to making money online, leveraging the power of essential apps can significantly enhance your chances of success. These apps offer a range of capabilities, from improving productivity and organization to providing platforms for freelancing and monetizing your skills. Here are some of the essential apps that can help you make money online.

1. Freelancing Platforms: Platforms like Upwork, Fiverr, and Freelancer connect freelancers with clients seeking their skills. These apps provide a user-friendly interface, allowing you to create a profile, showcase your expertise, and bid on relevant projects. They cover a wide range of industries, including writing, design, programming, digital marketing, and more.

2. Online Marketplaces: Platforms such as Etsy, eBay, and Amazon provide opportunities for individuals to sell products online. Whether you have handmade crafts,

vintage items, or even new merchandise, these apps allow you to set up your online store, manage inventory, and reach a global customer base.

3. Money Management Apps: Proper financial management is crucial when making money online. Apps like Mint, QuickBooks, or FreshBooks help you track your income, expenses, and overall financial health. They provide tools for invoicing clients, setting budgets, and generating financial reports, helping you stay organized and make informed decisions.

4. Remote Work Collaboration Tools: When working with remote teams or clients, collaboration becomes essential. Apps like Slack, Microsoft Teams, and Trello support seamless communication, file sharing, and project management. These tools enhance productivity, ensure smooth workflow, and facilitate successful cooperation with others.

5. Online Learning Platforms: Developing new skills is crucial for online success. Platforms like Udemy, Coursera, and LinkedIn Learning provide a vast array of courses on various subjects. By honing your skills or acquiring new ones, you can increase your market value and attract higher-paying opportunities.

6. Social Media and Content Creation Apps: Building an online presence is essential for making money online. Utilizing apps such as Instagram, YouTube, or TikTok enables you to showcase your expertise, reach a wider audience, and potentially monetize your content through brand sponsorships, advertising, or affiliate marketing.

7. Virtual Meeting Apps: Virtual meetings and video conferences have become integral to online business. Apps like Zoom, Google Meet, or Microsoft Teams facilitate seamless and professional communication with

clients, collaborators, or employers, regardless of physical distance.

8. Cashback and Reward Apps: Maximizing your earnings also involves saving money on your online purchases. Apps like Honey, Rakuten, or Swagbucks offer cashback or reward programs, allowing you to earn money or redeem points while shopping online.

Remember, while these essential apps can enhance your online earning potential, success ultimately depends on your perseverance, dedication, and the unique value you bring to the digital marketplace. By leveraging these platforms effectively and continuously improving your skills, you can create a pathway towards financial success in the online world.

Chapter3

Leveraging Social Media Platforms:

Leveraging social media platforms has become essential for individuals and businesses looking to make money online. The power of social media lies in its ability to reach a wide audience and engage with potential customers. Here, I will discuss the essential apps that can help you maximize your earning potential on social media.

1. Facebook Ads Manager: Facebook is one of the largest social media platforms and offers a robust advertising platform through its Ads Manager. It allows you to create, manage, and optimize ad campaigns, targeting specific demographics, interests, and behaviors. The comprehensive analytics provided by Facebook Ads Manager enable you to track the effectiveness of your ads and make data-driven decisions to maximize your online earnings.

2. Instagram for Business: With over 1 billion active users, Instagram has become a powerful tool for businesses to monetize their online presence. The Instagram for Business app provides features like shoppable posts, Instagram Stories, and insights that allow you to promote your products or services effectively. By leveraging these tools, you can attract potential customers, drive traffic to your website, and increase your online revenue.

3. YouTube Creator Studio: YouTube has emerged as a lucrative platform for content creators to monetize their videos. The YouTube Creator Studio app provides valuable resources for managing your channel, tracking video performance, and optimizing your content. Through advertising revenue, sponsorships, and collaborations, YouTube creators can generate substantial income by leveraging the platform's broad user base.

4. Pinterest for Business: Pinterest is a visually-driven platform that can be a goldmine for businesses in various niches. The Pinterest for Business app offers tools and features specifically designed to enhance your online earning potential. By creating eye-catching pins, optimizing keywords, and utilizing Pinterest's advertising options, you can attract a highly engaged audience and drive traffic to your website or blog, ultimately generating revenue through affiliate marketing or product sales.

5. LinkedIn Sales Navigator: LinkedIn is the go-to platform for professionals across industries, making it an invaluable resource for networking and generating leads. The LinkedIn Sales Navigator app provides advanced search and messaging features that can help you connect with potential clients or customers. By building meaningful relationships and showcasing your expertise, you can effectively leverage

LinkedIn to increase your online earning potential.

In conclusion, leveraging social media platforms is crucial for making money online in today's digital landscape. By utilizing apps like Facebook Ads Manager, Instagram for Business, YouTube Creator Studio, Pinterest for Business, and LinkedIn Sales Navigator, you can optimize your presence on these platforms and tap into their vast potential to generate revenue. However, it's important to develop a strategic approach, consistently produce high-quality content, and engage with your audience to maximize your earning potential on social media.

Monetizing your Social Media Profiles:

Monetizing your social media profiles has become an essential avenue for making money online in today's digital landscape. With the ever-increasing popularity of platforms such as Facebook, Instagram, Twitter, and YouTube, individuals can leverage their online presence to generate substantial income streams. Here, I will delve into essential apps and strategies to help you effectively monetize your social media profiles.

1. Influencer Marketing Platforms: Joining influencer marketing platforms like Upfluence, Tribe, or GrapeVine can provide you with numerous opportunities to collaborate with brands. These platforms act as intermediaries between influencers and companies, connecting you with potential campaigns and sponsors who are willing to pay for sponsored content.

2. Affiliate Marketing Networks: Affiliate marketing is a powerful method to earn money from your social media profiles. By joining affiliate marketing networks such as Amazon Associates, ShareASale, or Commission Junction, you can earn

commissions by promoting products or services. Affiliate links are generated, and you earn a percentage of each sale made through your unique links.

3. Sponsored Posts: Sponsored posts are an effective way to monetize your social media profiles. When you have a substantial following, brands may approach you for collaborations or sponsored content opportunities. By promoting a product or service and providing a compelling call-to-action, you can earn a fee for each sponsored post.

4. Content Creation Apps: Utilize content creation apps like Canva, Adobe Spark, or PicMonkey to enhance the quality of your posts. Eye-catching visuals and professional designs will not only attract more followers but also entice potential advertisers. These apps make it easy to create stunning graphics, infographics, and videos, adding value to your social media feed.

5. Social Media Management Tools: To effectively monetize your social media profiles, it is crucial to maintain a consistent and engaging presence. Apps like Hootsuite, Buffer, or Sprout Social can help you schedule posts, track analytics, and interact with your audience efficiently. By streamlining your social media management, you can optimize your content strategy and increase the chances of monetization opportunities.

6. YouTube Partnership Programs: If you have a YouTube channel, consider joining the YouTube Partner Program. This allows you to monetize your videos through ads, channel memberships, merchandise shelf, and super chat. As your channel grows, you can unlock additional features such as sponsorships and YouTube Premium revenue.

7. Crowdfunding Platforms: If you provide valuable content or have a creative project, crowdfunding platforms like Patreon or Kickstarter can be a great avenue for monetization. These platforms allow your followers to support you financially and receive exclusive benefits or early access to your content in return.

Remember, successful monetization of your social media profiles requires consistent and authentic engagement with your audience. Building a loyal following by providing value and creating compelling content is essential to attract brands and secure monetization opportunities. It is also crucial to comply with platform guidelines and disclose any sponsored content transparently to maintain credibility.

By leveraging the power of these essential apps and strategies, you can turn your social media profiles into profitable ventures,

capitalizing on your digital influence and generating a sustainable income online.
Becoming an Influencer:

Becoming an influencer has become a highly lucrative and sought-after profession in recent years. With the power of social media and the internet, individuals now have the opportunity to build their personal brand and monetize their influence. However, this career path requires dedication, strategy, and a deep understanding of the digital landscape. In this article, we will explore the essential steps to becoming a successful influencer.

1. Define Your Niche: To stand out in the crowded influencer world, it's crucial to find your niche. Choose a specific area of expertise or interest that aligns with your passions and strengths. By focusing on a niche, you can establish yourself as an authority and build a dedicated follower base.

2. Create High-Quality Content: Content is king in the digital realm. Invest in creating high-quality content that resonates with your target audience.

Whether it's captivating photos, engaging videos, or insightful blog posts, ensure that your content is visually appealing, informative, and relevant. Consistency is key - regularly post content to keep your audience engaged and interested.

3. Build a Strong Personal Brand: Building a strong personal brand is vital to differentiate yourself from other influencers. Take the time to define your unique brand identity, including your values, personality, and style. Leverage social media platforms to showcase your brand, ensuring consistency in your tone, aesthetics, and messaging across different channels.

4. Engage and Interact with Your Audience: Engaging with your audience is pivotal to

cultivate a loyal following. Respond to comments, DMs, and inquiries promptly and authentically. Foster a sense of community by hosting Q&A sessions, running contests or giveaways, and initiating conversations with your followers. This interaction establishes trust, promotes loyalty, and encourages user-generated content.

5. Collaborate with Brands and Networking: Collaborating with brands is an effective way to monetize your influence. As your following grows, brands will be interested in partnering with you to promote their products or services. Approach brands that align with your niche and values, and propose meaningful collaboration ideas. Networking with fellow influencers, attending industry events, and joining influencer marketing platforms can expand your opportunities for partnerships.

6. Diversify Your Income Streams: Relying solely on brand collaborations may not provide a stable income. Explore additional revenue streams such as affiliate marketing, sponsored content, creating and selling digital products or merchandise, and offering consulting or coaching services. Diversifying your income sources mitigates risks and allows you to maximize your earnings.

7. Stay Updated and Adapt: The digital landscape is ever-evolving, so it's vital to stay updated with the latest trends, algorithms, and platform changes. Continuously educate yourself about social media marketing strategies, learn from successful influencers, and adapt your content and tactics accordingly. Embrace new platforms and emerging technologies to stay ahead of the game.

Becoming an influencer requires hard work, perseverance, and a smart strategy. By defining your niche, creating outstanding content, building a strong personal brand, engaging with your audience, collaborating with brands, diversifying your income streams, and staying adaptable, you can pave your way to a successful career as an influencer. Remember, authenticity, passion, and providing value to your audience are vital characteristics that will help you thrive in this competitive field.

Creating Engaging Content for Profit:

Creating engaging content is crucial for attracting and retaining an online audience, as well as generating profit from your efforts. Whether you are a blogger, social media influencer, or content creator, implementing certain strategies can help monetize your content effectively. Here are some essential tips for creating engaging content for profit:

1. Know Your Target Audience: Understanding your target audience's interests, preferences, and demographics is vital. Conducting thorough market research allows you to tailor your content to their specific needs and desires. By delivering content that resonates with your audience, you increase the likelihood of engagement and conversions.

2. Consistency is Key: Consistency in posting and maintaining a regular content schedule helps to build trust and expectation with your audience. Whether it's daily, weekly, or monthly, establish a consistent schedule to keep your audience engaged and coming back for more.

3. Craft Captivating Headlines: A catchy headline is the gateway to captivating content. Make sure your headlines are attention-grabbing, concise, and provide a clear indication of what readers can expect from the content. Consider using power

words, posing intriguing questions, or offering valuable solutions to pique the curiosity of your audience.

4. Quality Content Creation: It goes without saying that the quality of your content will significantly impact engagement levels. Provide informative, useful, and entertaining content that adds value to your audience's lives. Incorporate multimedia elements like images, videos, and infographics to enhance the visual appeal and engagement of your content.

5. Encourage Audience Interaction: Actively encourage your audience to engage with your content through comments, likes, shares, and retweets. Pose questions, encourage discussions, and respond to comments promptly to foster a sense of community and make your audience feel heard and valued.

6. Collaborate with Influencers: Partnering with influencers or industry experts can help you expand your reach and tap into their existing audience.

Collaborative content, such as interviews, guest posts, or joint projects, can create fresh and exciting content that attracts new followers and drives engagement.

7. Utilize SEO Techniques: Search engine optimization (SEO) is crucial for increasing your content's visibility and attracting organic traffic. Research relevant keywords and incorporate them strategically into your content, meta descriptions, and titles to improve search engine rankings, driving more traffic to your website or platform.

8. Diversify Monetization Channels: Explore various monetization channels based on your niche and content format. Options like affiliate marketing, sponsored posts, advertising networks, digital products

(eBooks, courses), and memberships can help you generate income from your engaging content.

9. Analyze and Adapt: Regularly analyze your content performance using web analytics tools to gain insights into what works and what doesn't. Monitor engagement metrics, such as bounce rates, time on page, and social shares. Use this data to refine your content strategy and make data-driven decisions for future content creation.

Remember, creating engaging content for profit requires time, effort, and a deep understanding of your target audience's preferences. By consistently providing high-quality content, encouraging interaction, and diversifying your revenue streams, you can effectively monetize your online presence and turn your passion into a profitable venture.

Chapter4

Exploring E-Commerce Opportunities:

In recent years, the rise of smartphones has revolutionized not only the way we communicate and access information but also how we conduct business. In particular, the advent of e-commerce has opened up a plethora of opportunities for individuals looking to make money online. With the convenience and portability of smartphones, entrepreneurs and freelancers can easily tap into this growing market, capitalizing on the power of mobile technology to fuel their financial success.

To effectively explore e-commerce opportunities on smartphones, it is crucial to identify the essential apps that can facilitate and enhance your online business initiatives. These apps serve as invaluable tools, providing a range of features and functionalities aimed at optimizing your productivity, sales, and overall performance. Let's delve into some of the key apps that can help you make money online through e-commerce.

1. E-commerce Platforms:
One of the fundamental elements in establishing an online business is choosing the right e-commerce platform. Several popular platforms, such as Shopify, WooCommerce, and Magento, offer dedicated mobile apps that allow you to manage your store, track sales, process orders, and communicate with customers directly from your smartphone. These user-friendly interfaces enable you to easily set up, customize, and maintain your online store, making it accessible to potential customers worldwide.

2. Payment Gateway Apps:
To facilitate secure and seamless financial transactions, integrating a reliable payment gateway is essential. Consider using apps

like PayPal, Stripe, or Square, which enable you to accept payments from customers, send invoices, and manage your finances. These apps offer features like recurring billing, invoicing, and robust security measures, ensuring that your transactions are transparent and protected.

3. Social Media and Marketing Apps:
Leveraging social media platforms is crucial in driving traffic, building brand awareness, and increasing sales for your e-commerce business. Apps like Facebook Pages Manager, Instagram Business, and LinkedIn can help you effectively manage your social media presence. These apps allow you to schedule posts, engage with your audience, analyze insights, and run advertisements, empowering you to reach a wider customer base and boost your online revenue.

4. Inventory Management Apps:
Proper inventory management is vital for any e-commerce business to stay organized

and meet customer demands. With apps such as Stock and Inventory Management, Ordoro, or TradeGecko, you can effectively track your inventory levels, manage orders, and generate reports. These apps automate tasks like stock updates, order fulfillment, and backorder management, ensuring that you can efficiently handle the logistics side of your online business.

5. Analytics and Performance Tracking Apps:
Measuring and analyzing your e-commerce performance is essential for making informed business decisions. Utilize apps like Google Analytics, Adobe Analytics, or Hotjar to gain insights into customer behavior, website traffic, conversion rates, and other key performance indicators. These apps provide comprehensive reports and visualizations, enabling you to identify strengths, weaknesses, and opportunities for growth.

In conclusion, smartphones present an unparalleled opportunity for individuals to explore and capitalize on e-commerce ventures. By leveraging essential apps tailored for online business, you can effectively manage your store, process payments, market your products or services, and monitor your performance – all from the convenience of your smartphone. Embrace technology, harness the power of e-commerce, and unlock your potential to make money online through these indispensable apps.

Starting an Online Store:

Starting an online store can be an exciting and lucrative venture in today's digital age. With the increasing popularity of e-commerce, there are vast opportunities to establish a successful business and generate a steady income. However, it is essential to approach this endeavor strategically and with careful consideration. Here are some key steps to follow when starting your own online store.

1. Define your niche: Before diving into the world of online retail, it is crucial to identify your target market and niche. Research various product categories and explore gaps or trends that can differentiate your store from competitors. By focusing on a specific niche, you can effectively tailor your offerings and marketing strategies to attract the right customers.

2. Conduct market research: Thoroughly analyze your target market and identify your potential customers' preferences, needs, and purchasing behavior.

This research will enable you to make informed decisions about product selection, pricing, and marketing strategies. Additionally, it will assist in identifying potential competitors and understanding their strengths and weaknesses.

3. Choose the right platform: There are numerous e-commerce platforms available that provide user-friendly interfaces and comprehensive tools for setting up an online store. Consider factors such as cost, customization options, scalability, and integration with other essential services, such as payment gateways and shipping providers. Popular platforms include Shopify, WooCommerce, and BigCommerce, among others.

4. Develop a visually appealing website: Design an attractive and user-friendly website that reflects your brand identity and resonates with your target audience. Optimize it for both desktop and mobile devices, ensuring a seamless browsing and purchasing experience. The website should be easy to navigate, have well-organized product categories, and display high-quality product images and detailed descriptions.

5. Source your products: Determine your sourcing strategy, whether it be manufacturing your own products, establishing partnerships with suppliers, or utilizing dropshipping. Conduct due diligence to ensure product quality, reliability, and competitive pricing. Building strong relationships with suppliers is vital for maintaining inventory consistency and meeting customer demands.

6. Implement a robust marketing strategy: A successful online store relies heavily on effective marketing strategies to drive traffic and convert visitors into customers. Utilize digital marketing channels, such as search engine optimization, social media marketing, content marketing, email marketing, and influencer collaborations, to increase your online visibility and reach your target audience. Additionally, consider offering promotions, discounts, and loyalty programs to incentivize customer engagement and repeat purchases.

7. Streamline backend operations: Optimize your store's backend operations to ensure a smooth customer experience. Implement streamlined order management systems, secure payment gateways, and efficient shipping and fulfillment processes. Customer service should be a priority, with prompt responses to inquiries and a hassle-free return and exchange policy.

8. Monitor and analyze performance: Regularly track and analyze key performance indicators (KPIs) to evaluate the effectiveness of your store's performance. Monitor metrics such as website traffic, conversion rates, average order value, customer acquisition costs, and customer retention. This data will provide valuable insights into areas that need improvement and enable you to make data-driven decisions for sustained growth.

Starting an online store requires careful planning, diligent execution, and continuous adaptation to market trends and customer preferences. By following these steps and staying committed to delivering value to your customers, you can establish a successful and profitable online retail business.

Dropshipping and Affiliate Marketing:

Dropshipping and affiliate marketing are two popular methods for making money online. They both offer the opportunity to earn an income from the comfort of your own home, and have become increasingly popular in recent years. In this article, we will explore the essential apps that can help you succeed in these online business ventures.

1. Shopify: When it comes to dropshipping, Shopify is the go-to platform. It allows you to easily set up your online store, manage

inventory, and process orders. Shopify offers various themes and customization options to create a professional and visually appealing storefront. The platform integrates with numerous third-party apps and tools, making it a versatile choice for dropshipping business owners.

2. Oberlo: Linked directly to Shopify, Oberlo empowers dropshippers by streamlining the process of finding and adding products to their online store.
The app connects you with reputable suppliers and enables you to import product listings, images, and descriptions with just a few clicks. Oberlo also handles inventory and price updates automatically, eliminating the need for manual adjustments.

3. AliExpress: As one of the largest global marketplaces, AliExpress is a treasure trove for dropshippers. It offers an extensive range of products at competitive prices, making it the ideal platform for sourcing

inventory. With seamless integration with Oberlo, you can easily import products from AliExpress to your Shopify store, simplifying the dropshipping process.

4. Amazon Associates: For those exploring affiliate marketing, Amazon Associates is a must-have app. It allows you to earn commission by promoting products from the vast Amazon catalog. With Amazon's credibility and extensive product selection, affiliates can tap into a wide range of categories to find products that align with their niche and target audience. The affiliate program provides detailed reporting, tracking links, and various promotional tools to help maximize your earnings.

5. ClickBank: ClickBank is a popular affiliate network that specializes in digital products. It offers a wide range of categories, from health and fitness to personal development and e-commerce. Affiliates can easily find products to promote, as ClickBank provides

detailed sales statistics, gravity scores, and commission rates. The platform also ensures timely payments to affiliates, making it a reliable choice for earning passive income.

6. Google AdSense: If you have a blog or website, Google AdSense is a valuable tool for monetizing your content through contextual advertising. By placing relevant ads on your site, you can earn revenue based on user engagement and ad clicks. Google AdSense optimizes ad placement and provides detailed analytics to help you enhance your monetization strategy. It's a popular choice for bloggers and content creators looking to generate income from their online platforms. Dropshipping and affiliate marketing are lucrative online business opportunities that can be pursued with the help of essential apps. Shopify, Oberlo, AliExpress, Amazon Associates, ClickBank, and Google AdSense are key tools that can streamline your business

operations and maximize your earnings. By leveraging these apps effectively, you can build a successful online business and tap into the vast potential of the digital marketplace.

Maximizing Sales through Mobile Marketing:

This has become essential in today's digital landscape. With the increasing popularity of smartphones and the constant connectivity they provide, businesses have the opportunity to reach and engage with their target audience like never before. To make the most of this potential, it is crucial to leverage essential apps for mobile marketing. These apps can help businesses optimize their sales strategies, drive conversions, and enhance customer experiences.

1. Mobile Advertising Platforms: Utilizing mobile advertising platforms like Google

Ads and Facebook Ads can significantly boost sales. These platforms offer advanced targeting options, allowing businesses to reach their desired audience based on demographics, interests, and behaviors. By crafting compelling ad campaigns and optimizing them for mobile devices, businesses can drive traffic to their websites or mobile apps, ultimately leading to increased sales.

2. Mobile Analytics Tools: Implementing mobile analytics tools such as Google Analytics or Mixpanel can provide valuable insights into user behavior, preferences, and conversion rates. These tools track app or website usage, allowing businesses to identify bottlenecks, optimize their sales funnels, and make data-driven decisions. By understanding customer behavior and preferences, businesses can tailor their offers and promotions to maximize sales.

3. Mobile Payment Gateways: Integrating mobile payment gateways like PayPal, Stripe, or Apple Pay can enhance the purchasing process, simplifying transactions for customers. These secure and convenient payment options help reduce friction during checkout, leading to higher conversion rates. By offering a seamless and user-friendly payment experience, businesses can increase sales and enhance customer satisfaction.

4. Mobile CRM Apps: Implementing Customer Relationship Management (CRM) apps designed for mobile devices can streamline sales processes and improve customer interactions. These apps allow businesses to manage leads, track interactions, and nurture customer relationships on the go. By having access to customer data, sales teams can personalize their approach, provide timely follow-ups, and ultimately increase conversions.

5. Mobile Communication Tools: Utilizing mobile communication tools like WhatsApp Business or Slack can improve customer engagement and support. These apps offer real-time messaging capabilities, allowing businesses to address customer inquiries promptly and provide personalized assistance. By delivering excellent customer service and building rapport, businesses can boost customer loyalty, resulting in repeat sales.

6. Mobile Coupon and Loyalty Programs: Deploying mobile coupon and loyalty program apps can incentivize customers to make purchases and foster long-term relationships. These apps enable businesses to offer exclusive discounts, rewards, and personalized incentives directly to customers' mobile devices. By leveraging these programs, businesses can encourage repeat purchases, increase customer retention, and ultimately drive sales growth.

In summary, optimizing sales through mobile marketing requires leveraging essential apps that facilitate effective advertising, enable efficient payment processes, provide valuable analytics, enhance customer interactions, and foster loyalty. By incorporating these apps into their mobile marketing strategies, businesses can maximize sales, connect with their target audience, and establish a competitive edge in the online marketplace.

Chapter5

Making the Most of Online Freelancing:

In today's digital age, the versatility and flexibility of online freelancing have made it a lucrative avenue for individuals seeking to make a living from the comfort of their own homes. With the right skills, mindset, and tools at your disposal, you can maximize your potential and make the most of this ever-growing field. To help you achieve success in online freelancing, here are some essential tips and practices to consider:

1. Identify your niche: To stand out in the competitive world of online freelancing, it is crucial to identify a niche that aligns with your skills and expertise. Specializing in a specific area allows you to position yourself as an expert and attract clients seeking your specific services. Whether it's web development, graphic design, writing, or social media management, finding your

niche is the foundation for creating a successful freelancing career.

2. Build a professional online presence: Establishing a strong online presence is key to attracting clients and showcasing your skills.

Create a professional website or portfolio to showcase your previous work, highlight your accomplishments, and display testimonials from satisfied clients. Utilize social media platforms, such as LinkedIn or Twitter, to network with potential clients and engage with industry professionals. Additionally, consider joining relevant online communities or forums to expand your network and gain exposure.

3. Polish your skills and continuously learn: The online freelancing landscape is ever-evolving, and staying up-to-date with the latest industry trends and technologies is crucial for remaining competitive. Invest

in professional development by taking online courses, attending workshops, or joining webinars to enhance your existing skill set. Constantly refining your skills will not only boost your confidence but also attract higher-paying clients who value expertise and innovation.

4. Price your services appropriately: Determining your rates can be challenging, especially for freelancers starting out.
Research market rates and factor in your experience, expertise, and the value you bring to the table. While it can be tempting to undercut your competition to secure clients, it's essential to price your services in a way that reflects your worth. Remember, quality work often commands a higher price, and clients who are willing to pay for it are more likely to offer repeat business and referrals.

5. Utilize freelance platforms: Freelance platforms serve as a valuable resource for

finding clients and securing projects. Platforms such as Upwork, Freelancer, or Fiverr provide a platform for freelancers to connect with clients from around the world. Create a compelling profile, tailor your proposals to showcase your expertise, and leverage the platform's tools and resources to optimize your chances of success. However, it's important to note that competition can be fierce, so it's essential to make your profile and proposals stand out.

In conclusion, online freelancing offers endless opportunities for individuals looking to make money remotely. By identifying your niche, building a professional online presence, continuously improving your skills, pricing your services appropriately, and utilizing freelance platforms, you can maximize your potential and thrive in the world of online freelancing. Remember, consistent effort, dedication, and a commitment to excellence are crucial for long-term success in this dynamic field.

Finding Freelance Opportunities:

This is essential for those looking to make money online. Whether you are a seasoned freelancer or just getting started, it is crucial to explore various avenues and platforms to maximize your earning potential. Here are some essential apps and platforms that can help you find lucrative freelance gigs:

1. Upwork: Upwork is one of the most popular platforms for freelancers, offering a wide range of job categories to choose from. It allows you to create a profile highlighting your skills and experience, and bid on relevant projects. With a vast user base, Upwork provides ample opportunities to connect with clients worldwide.

2. Fiverr: Fiverr is another well-known platform that allows freelancers to offer their services across different categories or "gigs." From graphic design and writing to

programming and marketing, you can showcase your expertise and attract potential clients.

Fiverr also encourages building a strong portfolio to enhance your credibility.

3. Freelancer: Freelancer is a competitive marketplace where freelancers can find a vast array of projects. Registering on the platform enables you to bid on projects that match your skillset. Make sure to optimize your profile to stand out among other freelancers and gain visibility among clients.

4. Toptal: If you are a highly skilled professional looking for premium freelance opportunities, Toptal might be the right platform for you. Toptal focuses on connecting freelancers with top-tier clients in fields like software development, design, and finance. The platform has a rigorous screening process to ensure the quality of freelancers.

5. Guru: Guru offers a user-friendly interface for freelancers across various industries. You can create a profile, showcase your work, and bid on available projects. The platform offers different membership levels, each providing additional benefits such as more bids per month and improved visibility.

6. LinkedIn: While not traditionally thought of as a freelance platform, LinkedIn can be a valuable resource for finding freelance opportunities. Connect with professionals in your industry, join relevant groups, and engage in discussions. Many employers and recruiters also post freelance projects on the platform, so keeping an eye on job listings can be beneficial.

In addition to using these platforms and apps, actively networking and building a strong online presence is essential. Leverage social media platforms like Twitter and

Instagram to showcase your work, engage with potential clients, and keep up with industry trends. Additionally, consider reaching out to local businesses or exploring niche job boards specific to your skills.

Remember, success as a freelancer requires perseverance, dedication, and continuous improvement of your skills. Combine the power of these essential apps with your expertise and proactive approach, and you will be well on your way to finding lucrative freelance opportunities online.

Building a strong freelance profile:

This is essential for success in the ever-expanding world of online work. A well-crafted profile not only increases your chances of securing projects but also showcases your skills and expertise to potential clients. Here are some key tips to help you establish a compelling freelance profile:

1. Choose a professional platform: Research and select a reputable freelance platform that aligns with your skills and target audience. Platforms like Upwork, Freelancer, or Fiverr are popular choices. Ensure that the platform offers the features and opportunities that are relevant to your field and desired level of engagement.

2. Craft a captivating headline: Your headline is your first impression. Use it to convey your area of expertise, highlighting the value you bring to clients.

For example, instead of a generic "Freelance Writer," consider something like "Wordsmith Extraordinaire Delivering Engaging Content."

3. Write a compelling bio: Your bio should be concise, engaging, and articulate your skills, experience, and uniqueness. Focus on your strengths and the specific services you

offer. Provide concrete examples or notable achievements to establish credibility. Use keywords related to your niche to make your profile more discoverable in search results.

4. Showcase your portfolio: A strong portfolio is crucial in demonstrating your abilities and attracting potential clients. Include your best work examples that are relevant to your target clients. Showcase a diverse range of projects to highlight your versatility. If you're just starting out, consider offering pro bono work or personal projects to build your portfolio.

5. Highlight testimonials and reviews: Positive feedback from previous clients is a powerful tool in building trust. Request testimonials from satisfied clients and feature them prominently on your profile. If you're new to freelancing, consider offering discounted rates or delivering exceptional service to gather early positive feedback.

6. Display your professional image: Use a high-quality and professional profile photo that reflects your brand. Dress appropriately and maintain a friendly yet professional demeanor in any accompanying images or videos. Clients appreciate a freelancer who presents themselves in a polished and reliable manner.

7. Emphasize your communication skills: Clear and prompt communication is key to successful freelancing.

Highlight your ability to effectively communicate with clients, meet deadlines, and manage expectations. This will give potential clients confidence in your ability to deliver high-quality work.

8. Continuously update and optimize: Regularly review and refine your profile based on client feedback and industry trends. Update your portfolio with new projects, refine your bio, and add any

relevant certifications or additional skills you acquire. Continual improvement showcases your dedication to your craft and keeps your profile fresh and appealing.

Building a strong freelance profile takes time and effort, but a well-crafted profile can help you attract high-quality clients, increase your earning potential, and establish your reputation in the online freelance community.

Managing Clients and Earning Potential:

In today's digital landscape, the potential for making money online is virtually limitless. As more individuals and businesses are embracing the internet as a platform for conducting various activities, it is essential to maximize your earning potential while effectively managing your clients. Whether you are providing freelance services, operating an e-commerce store, or running an online consultancy, employing the right strategies is crucial for long-term success.

To achieve success in managing clients and maximizing your earning potential online, consider the following essential steps:

1. Identify and Target Your Niche: Before diving into the online marketplace, it is crucial to identify your niche and understand your target audience.

Specializing in a specific area allows you to cater to the needs and preferences of a particular group, making it easier to position yourself as an expert and attract the right clients. Conduct market research and analyze competition to gain insights into potential opportunities and gaps in the market.

2. Build Strong Online Presence: Establishing a strong online presence is imperative for both attracting clients and

building credibility. Craft a professional website that showcases your skills, services, and testimonials from satisfied clients. Leverage social media platforms to engage with your target audience, share valuable content, and establish yourself as a thought leader in your field. Implement effective search engine optimization (SEO) techniques to rank higher on search engine results pages, improving your online visibility.

3. Foster Effective Communication: Clear, professional, and timely communication is vital for managing clients efficiently. Establish a streamlined communication process, such as using email, instant messaging platforms, or project management tools, to ensure seamless interaction with clients. Respond promptly to inquiries, provide regular updates on project progress, and maintain transparency to build trust and retain clients for the long term.

4. Set Clear Expectations: Clearly define project scope, timelines, deliverables, and pricing to avoid misunderstandings and discrepancies. A comprehensive service agreement or statement of work can provide clarity and protect both parties' interests. Regularly communicate progress and milestones to manage expectations effectively and ensure client satisfaction.

5. Provide Exceptional Customer Service: Excellent customer service is crucial in the online business world. Go the extra mile to deliver exceptional service, exceeding your clients' expectations. Promptly address any issues, resolve conflicts amicably, and maintain a positive and professional attitude throughout the client relationship. Satisfied clients are more likely to recommend your services, leading to increased earning potential through referrals.

6. Diversify Your Income Streams: To maximize your earning potential online, consider diversifying your income streams. Instead of relying solely on one source of income, explore additional opportunities within your niche.

This could involve creating and selling digital products, offering online courses or coaching services, or collaborating with other experts in joint ventures. By diversifying your income, you can tap into multiple revenue streams, increasing your earning potential.

7. Continuously Upgrade Your Skills: The online business landscape is ever-evolving, requiring you to stay abreast of the latest trends and developments in your industry. Invest in your professional development by attending webinars, workshops, and online courses to upgrade your skills and knowledge. This positions you as a valuable resource to clients and allows you to

increase your earning potential by offering specialized services.

By effectively managing clients and strategically maximizing your earning potential online, you can build a successful and sustainable online business. Remember, consistency, professionalism, and a client-centered approach are key factors in establishing long-lasting relationships and achieving financial success in the digital realm.

Chapter6

Unlocking the Power of Mobile Advertising:

This is a crucial endeavor for businesses in today's technologically-driven world. As mobile devices have become an integral part of our daily lives, reaching consumers through these channels has proven to be one of the most effective and efficient methods of promoting products and services.

Mobile advertising offers a unique opportunity for businesses to connect with their target audience on a personal level. With the vast majority of people carrying smartphones or tablets, the potential reach of mobile advertising is unparalleled. By leveraging the power of mobile devices, businesses can deliver targeted and personalized ads to individuals while they are on the go, capturing their attention in real-time.

One of the key advantages of mobile advertising is its ability to provide location-based targeting. Through GPS technology, businesses can target ads specifically to individuals in certain geographic locations.

This allows for highly relevant and contextually appropriate ads, increasing the likelihood of engagement and conversion. For example, a local restaurant can target potential customers in the vicinity with a timely offer, enticing them to visit and dine in.

Moreover, mobile advertising provides rich multimedia capabilities, enabling businesses to create engaging and interactive ad experiences. With high-resolution screens, audio capabilities, and touch interactions, businesses can create visually stunning and immersive ads that capture the attention of users. This not only enhances brand awareness but also drives higher levels of engagement and brand recall.

Another significant advantage of mobile advertising is the ability to leverage data and targeting options to reach the right audience. Businesses can tap into user data such as demographics, interests, and browsing behavior to deliver ads that are highly relevant to individual users. This level of personalization ensures that users are presented with ads that align with their interests and needs, increasing the likelihood of conversion. Advanced targeting options also allow businesses to serve ads across various mobile apps and websites, maximizing the exposure and reach of their campaigns.

To fully unlock the power of mobile advertising, it is crucial for businesses to adopt a data-driven approach. By continuously analyzing campaign data, businesses can gain insights into user behaviors, preferences, and trends, enabling them to refine their targeting strategies and optimize their ad placements. This iterative process allows businesses to continually improve the effectiveness and efficiency of their mobile advertising efforts, ultimately driving better results and return on investment.

In conclusion, mobile advertising offers businesses a powerful tool to reach and engage with their target audience effectively. By harnessing the advantages of location-based targeting, rich multimedia capabilities, data-driven insights, and personalized experiences, businesses can unlock the full potential of mobile advertising. Embracing this dynamic and ever-evolving advertising landscape can lead to increased brand visibility, engagement, and ultimately, business growth.

Understanding Mobile Advertising Platforms

Mobile advertising platforms have become a powerful tool for businesses to reach and engage with their target audience in the fast-paced world of mobile devices. These platforms enable businesses to unlock the power of mobile advertising by providing them with the means to effectively deliver their brand messages to mobile users.

Mobile advertising platforms offer a wide range of features and capabilities that help businesses optimize their mobile advertising campaigns. These platforms allow businesses to target specific demographics, interests, and locations, ensuring that their ads reach the right audience at the right time. By utilizing advanced targeting and tracking technologies, businesses can maximize the efficiency and effectiveness of their mobile ad campaigns.

One key advantage of mobile advertising platforms is their ability to leverage the rich capabilities of mobile devices. With features like location-based targeting, businesses can deliver hyper-localized ads to users based on their geographical location.

This enables businesses to deliver relevant and personalized advertisements that resonate with the target audience, increasing the chances of engagement and conversion.

Moreover, mobile advertising platforms provide businesses with a range of ad formats that can be tailored to suit their specific objectives. Whether it's display ads, video ads, native ads, or interactive ads, these platforms offer a variety of options to captivate users and drive desired actions. The ability to customize ad formats ensures that businesses can effectively communicate their brand message and capture the attention of mobile users.

Additionally, mobile advertising platforms offer comprehensive measurement and analytics tools to track the performance of ad campaigns. This enables businesses to gain valuable insights into user behavior, ad engagement, and conversion rates. Armed with data-driven insights, businesses can optimize their campaigns, refine targeting strategies, and improve overall ROI.

Understanding mobile advertising platforms is crucial for businesses looking to unlock the power of mobile advertising. These platforms provide businesses with the tools and capabilities to reach their target audience effectively, deliver personalized ad experiences, and track campaign performance. By leveraging the potential of mobile advertising platforms, businesses can harness the full potential of mobile advertising to drive brand awareness, engagement, and conversions in the digital age.

Creating Effective Mobile Ads:

In today's digital age, mobile advertising has become an essential component of any successful online marketing strategy. With people spending more time on their smartphones, reaching out to potential customers through mobile ads can yield significant financial benefits. If you're looking for easy ways to make money online, here are some effective tips for creating captivating mobile ads:

1. Understand Your Audience: Before crafting any ad, it's crucial to have a deep understanding of your target audience. Identify their demographics, interests, and preferences to tailor your ads specifically to their needs. This understanding will enhance the relevance and effectiveness of your mobile ads, ultimately increasing your chances of making money.

2. Keep it Simple and Eye-Catching: Mobile ads need to capture attention quickly, as users have limited screen space and a shorter attention span. Create visually appealing ads with minimal text and vibrant colors to make them stand out. Use concise and compelling messaging that conveys your value proposition clearly within seconds. This will maximize your chances of engaging potential customers and driving conversions.

3. Utilize Responsive Design: One of the keys to successful mobile ads is responsiveness. Ensure that your ads are designed to adapt to different mobile devices and screen sizes. A mobile-responsive design will provide a seamless experience for users across various devices, increasing the chances of ad engagement and ultimately, monetization.

4. Incorporate a Clear Call-to-Action: To generate revenue, your mobile ads must

have a strong and concise call-to-action (CTA). Whether it's urging users to make a purchase, sign up for a newsletter, or download an app, make sure your CTA is prominently displayed and easy to understand. It should motivate users to take the desired action, leading them to the next step in your sales funnel.

5. Leverage Mobile-Friendly Landing Pages: When users tap on your mobile ad, they should be directed to a mobile-optimized landing page that seamlessly matches the ad's promise. Ensure that the landing page is fast-loading, easy to navigate, and delivers the expected value. A seamless transition from ad to landing page will minimize bounce rates and encourage users to explore further and potentially convert, thus increasing your online earnings.

6. Test and Optimize: To maximize the monetization potential of your mobile ads, it's essential to test different variations and

optimize your campaigns continuously. Experiment with different ad formats, visuals, copy, and placements to identify what works best for your target audience. Continually review and analyze ad performance metrics, such as click-through rates (CTR) and conversion rates. Make data-driven decisions and refine your ads based on the insights gained from these metrics.

7. Monitor Competitors and Industry Trends: Stay updated with the latest trends and techniques in mobile advertising. Keep an eye on your competitors to gain inspiration and insight into what's working in your industry. By staying knowledgeable about the dynamic landscape of mobile ads, you can adapt your strategies, remain competitive, and increase your chances of making money online.

Creating effective mobile ads that generate revenue requires a thorough understanding of your audience, visually enticing designs, clear and compelling CTAs, mobile-responsive landing pages, continuous testing, and industry awareness. By implementing these strategies, you can improve the performance of your mobile ads and take advantage of the vast opportunities available to make money online.

Optimizing Ad Campaigns for Maximum ROI:

Running effective ad campaigns is crucial for businesses aiming to maximize their return on investment (ROI) in the digital landscape. To optimize ad campaigns and achieve superior results, it is important to employ strategic techniques that align with your target audience and business objectives. Here are some key tactics to consider for maximizing your ROI:

1. Define Clear Goals: Begin by setting clear and specific goals for your ad campaign.

Whether it's increasing brand awareness, driving website traffic, generating leads, or boosting sales, having well-defined goals will guide your optimization efforts.

2. Understand Your Target Audience: Do thorough research to identify your target audience's demographics, interests, and online behavior. Utilize tools like customer surveys, social media analytics, and market research to tailor your ad campaign to effectively reach and engage your ideal customers.

3. Choose the Right Advertising Channels: With countless advertising channels available, it's essential to identify the platforms that align with your target audience. Consider factors like user demographics, engagement levels, and ad formats offered by each platform. Popular choices include search engines (such as Google Ads), social media networks (like Facebook Ads), and mobile ad networks.

4. A/B Testing: Implement A/B testing to compare different versions of your ads, landing pages, and calls-to-action. This technique allows you to evaluate which variations perform better and helps refine your campaign to maximize ROI. Test various elements like ad copy, visuals, headlines, and targeting options to optimize your campaign's effectiveness.

5. Targeted Keyword Selection: If using search engine advertising, ensure your keyword selection is purposeful and aligned with your campaign goals. Conduct thorough keyword research to identify relevant search terms with adequate search volume but lower competition. This will help enhance visibility, increase click-through rates (CTR), and drive qualified traffic to your website.

6. Compelling Ad Creatives: Craft eye-catching and persuasive ad creatives

that effectively communicate your value proposition. Utilize compelling visuals, concise yet impactful copy, and strong calls-to-action to entice users to engage with your ad. Regularly experiment with different ad formats (text, image, video) to determine the most effective ones for your target audience.

7. Data-driven Optimization: Leverage analytics tools and tracking metrics to gather valuable insights on campaign performance. Monitor key performance indicators (KPIs) like CTR, conversion rate, engagement metrics, and cost-per-acquisition (CPA). Analyze this data regularly and make data-driven optimizations to refine your targeting, messaging, and ad placements for continuous improvement.

8. Conversion Optimization: Landing page optimization plays a pivotal role in maximizing your ad campaign's ROI.

Ensure that your landing pages are visually appealing, user-friendly, and optimized for mobile devices. Implement clear call-to-action buttons, minimize load times, and provide relevant content to enhance the chances of conversions.

9. Retargeting: Implementing retargeting campaigns can be highly effective in driving conversions among users who have previously shown interest in your brand or products. By reaching out to these warm leads via targeted ads across different platforms, you can reinforce brand awareness, re-engage potential customers, and increase the likelihood of conversions.

10. Ongoing Monitoring and Optimization: Continuously monitor and analyze your ad campaign performance to identify areas for improvement. Test and refine your strategy based on the insights gathered, industry trends, and user feedback. Regularly update your ad creatives, adjust targeting options,

and optimize bidding strategies to adapt to changes in your market and maximize ROI.

By implementing these optimization techniques, you can enhance the effectiveness of your ad campaigns, improve your ROI, and achieve greater success in the competitive world of online advertising.

Chapter7

Diving into App Development:

Unleashing Your Creativity and Building Your Profitable Ideas,
In today's digital era, app development has become an increasingly lucrative field, offering a multitude of opportunities for those looking to channel their creativity while making money online. Creating and launching a successful app can be a fulfilling venture that not only showcases your technical skills but also opens doors to significant financial returns.

To embark on the journey of app development, there are several key steps and strategies to keep in mind. By following these guidelines, you can maximize your chances of creating an effective and profitable mobile app.

1. Idea Generation and Market Research:

Start by brainstorming unique and innovative app ideas that have the potential to solve a problem or fulfill a need in the market. Conduct thorough market research to understand current trends, user preferences, and the competitive landscape. By identifying gaps or unmet demands, you can position your app for success.

2. User-Centric Design:
Designing a visually appealing and user-friendly interface is crucial to engage and retain users. Focus on creating an intuitive user experience that simplifies tasks, offers seamless navigation, and incorporates eye-catching graphics and animations. Incorporating user feedback during the design process can help you optimize the app for better usability.

3. Selecting the Right Platform:
Consider whether your app will be built for iOS, Android, or both. Analyze the target audience, market share, and revenue

potential of each platform. While launching on both platforms may broaden your reach, starting with one and gradually expanding can be a cost-effective approach, especially for beginners.

4. Working with Skilled Developers:
Whether you choose to learn coding yourself or hire a team of experienced developers, having skilled professionals on board is crucial. Collaborate with developers who specialize in the chosen app development platform, ensuring they have a track record of successful projects and can bring your ideas to life effectively.

5. Testing and Iteration:
Testing your app throughout the development process is essential to identify and fix any bugs or usability issues. Conduct beta testing with a group of users to gather their feedback and make necessary optimizations. Continually iterate and

improve your app based on the insights gained during this testing phase.

6. Monetization Strategies:
Consider the various monetization models available to make money from your app. Explore options such as in-app purchases, advertisements, subscriptions, or a premium version with additional features. Research industry standards and pricing to ensure that your app's monetization strategy aligns with users' expectations.

7. Marketing and Promotion:
Developing an exceptional app is just the first step; marketing and promotion are equally vital to achieve success. Create a comprehensive marketing plan that includes app store optimization (ASO), social media marketing, influencer collaborations, and targeted advertisements. Leverage various digital marketing channels to create buzz and generate downloads.

8. Analyzing User Feedback:

Once your app is live, pay close attention to user feedback and reviews. Analyze user behavior using analytics tools to gain insights into how users interact with your app and identify areas for improvement. Regularly update your app based on valuable user feedback to enhance user satisfaction and retention.

As you venture into app development, keep in mind that success requires dedication, ongoing learning, and adaptability. Stay up to date with the latest technologies, industry trends, and user expectations. By investing time and effort into the app development process, you can transform your creative ideas into a profitable online business.

Monetizing your App:

Monetizing your app is a crucial step in turning your hard work into a profitable venture. While there are various ways to generate revenue from your app, it is essential to choose the right strategy that aligns with your target audience, app niche, and long-term goals. Here are some effective ways to monetize your app:

1. In-App Advertising: Implementing ads within your app is one of the most common methods to monetize mobile applications. By integrating ad networks like Google AdMob or Facebook Audience Network, you can display banner ads, interstitials, or video ads to generate revenue based on impressions or clicks. However, it is important to strike a balance between user experience and ad placement to avoid frustrating or overwhelming your users.

2. Freemium Model: This model allows users to download your app for free while offering additional features or content through in-app purchases or subscriptions. Freemium models work well for apps that offer premium content, exclusive

functionalities, or an ad-free experience. It is important to offer meaningful value in the paid version to incentivize users to upgrade.

3. In-App Purchases: If your app offers virtual goods, additional levels, or exclusive content, you can implement in-app purchases to monetize these elements. Users can buy these items through microtransactions, creating a steady revenue stream. Ensure that the in-app purchases are not too pricey and provide genuine value to the users.

4. Sponsorship and Partnerships: Collaborating with relevant brands or businesses can be a profitable way to monetize your app. By offering sponsored content or partnering with companies whose products or services align with your app's theme, you can earn revenue through promotional campaigns, affiliate marketing, or referral programs. However, it is crucial to maintain the trust of your users by

selecting partners that genuinely benefit your audience.

5. Subscription Model: For apps that offer ongoing services, memberships, or access to exclusive content, a subscription-based model can be an effective way to monetize. Providing a free trial period or limited access can entice users to subscribe for continued access. Regularly update your app's content or features to create ongoing value for your subscribers.

6. Data Monetization: This monetization method involves collecting user data (anonymously and with user consent), analyzing it, and selling insights, trends, or targeted advertising based on the collected information. However, it is crucial to prioritize user privacy and adhere to legal and ethical guidelines when implementing this strategy.

7. Crowdfunding or Donations: If your app provides value to users without charging them directly, you can consider implementing a crowdfunding or donation option. This approach relies on voluntary contributions from users who appreciate your app's functionality or purpose. Engage with your community and clearly communicate how donations will be utilized to encourage support.

It is important to mention that the success of your app monetization strategy depends on factors such as user engagement, market demand, and the overall quality of your app. Understanding your target audience, tracking key metrics, and continuously iterating on your monetization approach will help you make informed decisions and maximize your revenue potential.

Promoting and Marketing Your App:

In today's highly competitive mobile app market, effectively promoting and marketing your app is crucial for its success. With millions of apps available across various app stores, you need to employ the right strategies to grab the attention of your target audience and stand out from the crowd. Here are some key steps to creating an effective app promotion and marketing campaign:

1. Define Your Target Audience: Before you start promoting your app, it's important to clearly identify your target audience. Understand their demographics, interests, and behaviors to tailor your marketing messages and select appropriate channels for promotion.

2. App Store Optimization (ASO): Optimizing your app's visibility in app stores is essential for increasing its discoverability. Conduct keyword research and include relevant keywords in your app's title,

description, and tags. Enhance your app's screenshots and icon to attract potential users. Regularly update your app to improve its ratings and reviews, which have a significant impact on search rankings.

3. Create Engaging App Landing Pages: Design compelling landing pages to showcase the key features and benefits of your app. Use persuasive language, visuals, and user testimonials to convince visitors to download your app. Include clear calls-to-action that prompt users to take immediate action and download your app.

4. Implement App Store Advertising: Consider investing in app store advertising to boost app visibility. Platforms like Google Ads and Apple Search Ads enable you to target specific keywords related to your app, increasing its visibility in search results. Run well-crafted ad campaigns to attract relevant users and drive downloads.

5. Utilize Social Media Marketing: Leverage the power of social media to create a buzz around your app. Identify platforms where your target audience is most active and engage with them regularly. Craft compelling content, including videos, images, and infographics, to showcase your app's features and benefits. Collaborate with influencers in your niche to extend your app's reach.

6. Implement Referral and Incentive Programs: Encourage your existing users to refer your app to their friends and family by offering referral rewards or incentives. This can significantly amplify your app's reach and generate organic downloads. Implement referral tracking mechanisms to track and reward successful referrals.

7. Leverage Influencer Marketing: Collaborate with popular influencers in your app's niche to promote your app. Influencers have a loyal fan base and can

create authentic content that resonates with their followers. This can drive significant downloads and increase your app's visibility within your target audience.

8. App Review Websites and Blogs: Reach out to popular app review websites and blogs to request reviews and featured listings for your app. Positive reviews and increased visibility on these platforms can help boost app downloads and credibility.

9. Measure and Optimize: Continuously monitor and analyze the performance of your app promotion and marketing efforts. Utilize app analytics tools to track user engagement, retention rates, and conversion rates. Identify areas of improvement and optimize your strategies accordingly.

Remember, effective app promotion and marketing require a mix of different strategies tailored to your app's target audience and niche. Be creative, stay updated with the latest trends, and constantly iterate your strategies to maximize the reach and impact of your app in the competitive mobile app market.

Exploring Passive Income Streams:

In today's digital age, the emergence of smartphones has revolutionized how we conduct business and explore various income-generating opportunities. Passive income streams have become an enticing avenue for individuals looking to earn money online. In this article, we will delve into the world of passive income and explore effective ways to generate income using smartphones.

1. Affiliate Marketing: One popular method to earn passive income on mobile devices is through affiliate marketing. This involves promoting products or services for companies and earning a commission for each sale or lead generated through your

referral link. Start by researching affiliate programs related to your niche, such as popular e-commerce platforms or mobile app developers. Create engaging and persuasive content to market these products effectively.

2. Mobile App Development: If you possess coding skills or have an interest in learning app development, creating and selling mobile applications can be a lucrative passive income stream. Identify gaps in the market or opportunities for innovative solutions. Develop apps that cater to specific needs or provide entertainment value. Monetize your app through in-app purchases, advertisements, or monthly subscriptions.

3. Content Creation: With the availability of high-quality smartphone cameras and user-friendly editing applications, creating and monetizing content has never been easier. Explore various platforms such as

YouTube, Instagram, or TikTok, and showcase your skills or knowledge in specific niches. Consistently produce valuable and engaging content that captures your audience's attention. As your following grows, you can monetize your content through brand partnerships, sponsored posts, or ad revenue.

4. Dropshipping: Running an online store without inventory has gained popularity in recent years. Using mobile devices, you can set up a dropshipping business by partnering with suppliers who handle order fulfillment. Choose trending or niche products and create an appealing online storefront. Optimize your website or mobile app for mobile users to ensure a seamless shopping experience. Drive traffic to your store through social media marketing, influencer collaborations, and targeted advertisements.

5. Stock Photography: If you have a passion for photography or possess a knack for capturing stunning visuals, consider selling your images on stock photography platforms. Mobile devices these days offer exceptional camera capabilities. Take high-quality photos and upload them to stock photo websites like Shutterstock or Adobe Stock. Each time someone purchases or licenses your photo, you earn a royalty fee.

6. Online Courses: With mobile devices as your tools, you can share your skills and knowledge by creating and selling online courses. Identify areas where you have expertise or experience and package your knowledge into a comprehensive course. Use popular e-learning platforms such as Udemy or Coursera to reach a wider audience. Optimize your course content for mobile viewing to cater to the increasing number of learners using smartphones.

In conclusion, exploring passive income streams on mobile devices presents an array of opportunities for individuals looking to make money online. Whether through affiliate marketing, mobile app development, content creation, dropshipping, stock photography, or online courses, leveraging your smartphone's capabilities can lead to a sustainable passive income. Remember, consistency, dedication, and continuous learning are key factors in achieving success in any passive income endeavor.

Chapter8

Conclusion:

By leveraging the incredible potential of your smartphone, you can unlock a world of opportunities to make money online. Creating effective mobile ads is a proven and accessible method that can lead to lucrative outcomes. When venturing into the realm of online earning, it is crucial to understand the importance of captivating and compelling advertisements that resonate with your target audience. By following the easy tips and strategies outlined in this guide, you can enhance your chances of success and maximize your profit potential. Remember to prioritize engaging visuals, concise messaging, and targeted marketing efforts. With dedication, creativity, and a solid understanding of your audience's needs, you can harness the power of your smartphone to generate income and achieve your financial goals. Get ready to embark on your journey towards a profitable online venture using your smartphone as your gateway to success.

Recap of Key Strategies for Making Money Online:

1. Identify your niche: Find a specific area or market that aligns with your interests, expertise, and target audience. This will allow you to establish yourself as an authority in that field and attract relevant customers.

2. Build an online presence: Create a professional website or blog to showcase your skills, products, or services. Use social media platforms to engage with your audience, share valuable content, and drive traffic to your online channels.

3. Monetize your skills: Determine how you can monetize your skills and knowledge. Consider offering freelance services,

creating digital products, or becoming an affiliate marketer for products or services that align with your niche.

4. Leverage digital advertising: Utilize various digital advertising platforms, such as Google AdSense or Facebook Ads, to promote your business and generate revenue. Understand your target audience's demographics and preferences to create effective and targeted advertisements.

5. Implement search engine optimization (SEO): Optimize your website and content for search engines to improve visibility and organic traffic. Use relevant keywords, publish high-quality content, and ensure your website is user-friendly and mobile-responsive.

6. Embrace affiliate marketing: Partner with reputable companies or brands and promote their products or services through affiliate links or referral programs. Earn

commissions for each successful sale or conversion generated from your platform.

7. Consider e-commerce: Explore the world of online retail by setting up an e-commerce store. Offer products or services directly to customers, manage inventory, and provide a seamless shopping experience.

8. Engage in online surveys and market research: Participate in online surveys and market research to earn small rewards or monetary compensation. Although it may not yield substantial income, it can generate some extra cash or gift cards.

9. Explore freelancing platforms: Register on freelancing platforms like Upwork or Fiverr to offer your skills and services to clients worldwide. This allows you to work on a flexible schedule and secure projects based on your expertise.

10. Develop digital courses or tutorials: Share your knowledge and expertise by creating and selling online courses or tutorials in your niche. Platforms like Udemy or Teachable provide an opportunity to monetize your skills while helping others learn.

Remember, making money online requires dedication, consistency, and continuous learning. Experiment with different strategies, adapt to market trends, and stay focused on providing value to your audience. With persistence and the right approach, you can leverage the power of the internet to generate a sustainable income stream.

The future of smartphone-monetization seems promising, with several key trends emerging on the horizon. The first trend we discussed is the rise of in-app purchases and freemium models as primary revenue streams, driven by the growing popularity of mobile gaming and app-based services. This shift towards a more user-centric and immersive experience is likely to continue, as developers find innovative ways to entice users to make in-app purchases.

Another important trend is the increasing emphasis on personalized and targeted advertising. As smartphones continue to evolve into highly personalized devices, advertisers will have more data at their disposal to deliver hyper-targeted ads to consumers. This trend aligns with the growing importance of mobile advertising, as marketers recognize the value of reaching users directly on their smartphones.

Furthermore, the integration of mobile payment systems and the continued growth of mobile commerce present significant opportunities for smartphone-monetization. With the rise of digital wallets and contactless payments, users are becoming more comfortable conducting financial transactions on their smartphones. This opens up new avenues for revenue generation, such as transaction fees and partnerships between smartphone manufacturers and financial institutions.

Lastly, the emergence of subscription-based services across various sectors, including music, video streaming, and cloud storage, is another trend to watch. The convenience and flexibility offered by subscription models have gained traction among consumers, providing a stable and recurring revenue stream for service providers. This trend is likely to continue as more industries recognize the benefits of offering subscription-based services through smartphone apps.

In summary, the future of smartphone-monetization is marked by the rise of in-app purchases, targeted advertising, mobile payments, and subscription-based services. These trends reflect a shift towards a more personalized and user-centric approach, as well as the increasing integration of smartphones into various aspects of our lives. Businesses that embrace these trends and adapt their monetization strategies accordingly are well-positioned to thrive in the evolving smartphone landscape.